Love, Inside & Out

Thoughtful Practices
for Creating a Kinder World

Anna Katz

Bluestreak
BOOKS

Bluestreak
Weldon Owen is a division of Bonnier Publishing USA
1045 Sansome Street, San Francisco, CA 94111
www.weldonowen.com

girl friday PRODUCTIONS

Edited and designed by Girl Friday Productions
www.girlfridayproductions.com

Written by Anna Katz

Library of Congress Cataloging-in-Publication data is available.

ISBN-13: 978-1-68188-258-1

First Printed in 2017
10 9 8 7 6 5 4 3 2 1
2017 2018 2019 2020

Printed in China

Introduction

Twenty-five hundred years ago, Chinese philosopher Laozi wrote, "Kindness in words creates confidence. Kindness in thinking creates profoundness. Kindness in giving creates love." Today's technologies and hairstyles may be different, but at our most basic level, people haven't changed that much. The advice for how to live happier, freer, more loving lives is fundamentally the same. In short: be kind.

This advice is both incredibly simple and surprisingly complex. There are as many ways to put love first as there are individuals on Earth—and an equal number of obstacles that get in love's way. Fear is one such obstacle, and like countless moments throughout history, now is a time when fear looms large.

Even when the whole world's gone mad, we can determine the state of our private inner worlds. If we get caught up in fear, we contract and contain, which ends up making our lives lonely and small.

But if we commit to kindness, we are able to foster a state of openness and curiosity that propels us to reach out into the wider world and invite others into our smaller one, to bridge the gap where misunderstanding is born. It comes down to a choice: fear or love?

And so it starts with you. It's up to you to decide whether you want to put love first and then think, speak, and act accordingly. It's up to you how big or small you want your expression of kindness to be, how far or close, how quiet or loud. In this journal you will find inspiring quotes and weekly exercises to help you think about and practice different forms of kindness through action, as well as kindness within through introspection and meditation. Some exercises involve practical opportunities, such as donating food to a food bank or giving pocket change to a person living on the street. Others are more relational, like saying hello to a stranger or reaching out to someone you've lost contact with. Still others involve expanding your own horizons and seeing where they might take you—for example, volunteering in your community or getting the news from a different news source than the one you usually use. Finally, there are exercises that encourage self-care, like making extra time for yourself or composing lists of things you are grateful for every day.

All of these exercises have the same agenda: to expand your compassion for the outer world and yourself. You can test them out any way you choose—go in order, skip around, return to one again and again and adapt it to make it your own. Every act of kindness—whether it's for yourself, your friends or family, your community, or the world at large—builds upon itself. When you act, in whatever form, with love, you are both *creating* and *being* love. And if you put love first, you have the power to be a force of kindness in an ever-changing world.

Say hello to a stranger every day this week.

It's easy to feel alone in this fast-paced world. Greeting someone you don't know can make an impression on both of you.

At the beginning of the week: How do you feel about saying hello to strangers? Do you tend to feel friendly or fearful toward them? What factors make you more open to greeting certain people than others?

Each time you say hello to a stranger, your heart acknowledges over and over again that we are all family.

SUZY KASSEM (B. 1975), WRITER,
FILMMAKER, AND CULTURAL CRITIC

Begin each day by paying yourself a compliment.

Whether you're proud of your work ethic, your marathon time, or your contagious laugh, pat yourself on the back each morning for one of the unique qualities that make you you.

At the beginning of the week: What is your self-talk usually like? Do you pay yourself compliments or are you critical of yourself? Write seven things about yourself that you like and pick one to focus on each day this week.

At the end of the week: Did you pay yourself a compliment each morning? Was it challenging or easy? How did beginning your day with positive self-talk affect you? Write about your most confident day this week and how the compliment you gave yourself might have changed your outlook.

Every day, find a quiet space where you can sit. If you don't already have a daily meditation practice, set a timer for five minutes. During that time, focus on your breath.

There are many good reasons to develop a meditation practice, including an improved ability to self-calm, which helps us think before we act. This, in turn, can allow us to choose to act from love. Pick a physical point to focus on—the pulling in and softening of your belly, the rise and fall of your chest, or the air as it moves in and out against the tip of your nose.

At the beginning of the week: What do you think about meditation? How does the thought of doing this exercise make you feel?

At the end of the week: Did you sit quietly for five minutes each day this week? What thoughts, feelings, and physical sensations did you experience? If you didn't do it, why not?

If you want others to be happy practice compassion. If you want yourself to be happy practice compassion.

14TH DALAI LAMA (B. 1935), SPIRITUAL LEADER

Commit to pausing before you react out of anger or frustration this week.

Maybe your daily commute spikes your anger, or you detest waiting in line at the grocery store or the bank. Next time you get angry, pause and consider what, if any, response is best. If you can practice on the smaller triggers first, then you might be better prepared the next time you're about to lash out in anger at someone in your life.

At the beginning of the week: What kind of situation makes you feel frustrated or angry? How do you usually react, both internally and externally? What do you think is the ideal response in this situation?

At the end of the week: Did you get angry or frustrated this week? How did you deal with your feelings? Are you proud of your reaction or would you go back and handle the situation differently if you could? Write about an effective way that you worked through your anger.

This week, call or text a friend you haven't spoken to recently.

You know that friend you've been meaning to call? Call her! Even if you only have time to send a text, you will brighten both her day and yours.

At the beginning of the week: Who have you fallen out of touch with? Why? How do you feel about reestablishing a connection? How do you think he or she will respond to your reaching out?

At the end of the week: Did you call or text a friend? Describe the interaction (or lack thereof). How did you feel after reconnecting or attempting to reconnect?

Every day, do something small but considerate for a stranger.

Extending a small kindness to someone is a simple way to make their life a little easier. It might mean giving up your seat on the train, holding the door open for someone, or helping someone reach a high shelf or carry something heavy. Whatever you choose to do, you'll be changing someone else's day for the better.

At the beginning of the week: Do you tend to help strangers? How might lending a hand in a small but considerate way affect your day? How might it influence theirs?

At the end of the week: Did you do something small but considerate for a stranger? How did you feel when you did so? Write about one interaction that stuck with you throughout the week.

Our task must be to free ourselves . . . by widening our circle of compassion.

ALBERT EINSTEIN (1879–1955),
THEORETICAL PHYSICIST

This week, publicly recognize someone who did something kind for you.

Did someone go out of their way for you recently? Let the world know you noticed! You might post about it on your social media or theirs, or send a group e-mail at work thanking them for their help.

At the beginning of the week: What act of kindness are you inspired to recognize? Describe how this act made you feel.

At the end of the week: Did you publicly recognize someone for their kindness? How did doing so make you feel? Did you receive a response? If so, what kind?

Write down three things you are grateful for each day this week.

Appreciating what you have—even when things are less than perfect—can make a big difference in your mood and your perception of your life.

At the beginning of the week: Consider how frequently you experience gratitude. Often? Rarely? What are some things that you feel grateful for on a regular basis? What are some things that you might take for granted?

At the end of the week: Did you make a gratitude list every day? How did it change your outlook at challenging times throughout the week? Did it affect your perceptions or behaviors?

Happiness quite unshared can scarcely be called happiness; it has no taste.

CHARLOTTE BRONTË (1816–1855),
NOVELIST AND POET

Do something for an animal this week.

Whether it's spending some extra time with your pet, volunteering with shelter animals, or donating to a wildlife conservation organization, you'll be helping animals and *humans. In fact, research shows that spending time with a furry friend can lower humans' blood pressure and increase oxytocin.*

At the beginning of the week: Write about the animals you encounter in your life—it could be your family dog, a cat you see around the neighborhood, birds at the park, or even the animals that make you smile on YouTube. What is something you can do to help an animal near or far?

At the end of the week: Did you contribute to the well-being of an animal or animals this week? If not, why not? If so, what did you do?

Every day, find a quiet space where you can just sit. Set a timer. During that time, focus on your breath.

Sitting quietly for a few minutes every now and then can have a positive impact on your life. And doing this consistently can have an even greater impact. Start with five minutes and then, if you're interested in a challenge, add some extra time to your practice. It doesn't have to be a lot—even two more minutes can make a difference.

At the beginning of the week: What is your experience with meditation? How does the thought of doing this exercise make you feel?

At the end of the week: Did you sit quietly each day this week? What thoughts, feelings, and physical sensations did you experience? Would you consider continuing this practice? If you didn't do it, what prevented you?

Spend time helping a community member this week.

Without expecting recognition or anything in return, go out of your way to help a neighbor or coworker. Give an elderly neighbor a ride to the grocery store and carry his groceries into his house, shovel the snow on a neighbor's sidewalk or mow the lawn on their parking strip, or clean the shared kitchen at work. Giving of your time to help someone in your community can go a long way.

At the beginning of the week: Do you tend to be aware of opportunities to help, or are you not always conscientious or willing to go out of your way to assist another? Think about your neighborhood, community, or workplace. Is there a neighbor who might need your help? Is there a task at work that no one wants to do? Write a list of some potential tasks you could do.

At the end of the week: Did you go above and beyond for someone this week? How did that make you feel? Were you able to do so without expecting anything in return, including recognition? If not, what do you think got in your way?

No act of kindness, no matter how small, is ever wasted.

AESOP (C. 620–564 BCE), FABULIST

Watch the news on TV, listen to a news podcast or radio program, or read the newspaper every day this week.

Not only is knowledge power, but knowing about the larger world can put your own challenges in perspective and spark compassion for others. You might even be inspired to learn more or get involved by calling an elected official or participating in a rally or march.

At the beginning of the week: What is one realm of current events you tend to avoid or about which you feel uninformed? Write about a current event you'd like to learn more about, including what you know about it already.

At the end of the week: Did you watch, listen, or read the news this week? Did you learn more about the current event you were interested in? Write about it here. Then write about one news item that surprised you or inspired you to get involved.

Treat yourself this week.

Big or small, free or expensive, doing something nice for yourself can simply feel good. Get a massage, go for a hike in the woods, visit the ice-cream shop for your favorite flavor of ice cream. When you feel good, it's natural to want to spread those feel-good vibes!

At the beginning of the week: When it comes to self-care, do you tend toward neglect or restraint? Or do you find it easy to treat yourself? Consider ways you can treat yourself and how you feel about it.

At the end of the week: Did you treat yourself this week? Do you think treating yourself affected the way you felt? Did it influence how you interacted with others?

When we give cheerfully and accept gratefully, everyone is blessed.

MAYA ANGELOU (1928–2014),
WRITER AND CIVIL RIGHTS ACTIVIST

Write a handwritten note to a family member or close friend this week.

Express your love to someone you cherish. Whether that person lives near or far, they'll appreciate knowing that you think enough about them to handwrite a note.

At the beginning of the week: Who are you going to write a loving note to this week? Why this person in particular? Write a rough draft here.

At the end of the week: Did you write a loving note to someone you care about this week? How did it make you feel? What kind of response, if any, did you receive?

This week, do something you've been putting off.

Whether it's organizing your pantry, doing your taxes, or finally hanging art up on your walls, there's always an excuse to put it off for tomorrow. But what if you did it today? Not only will it be a check mark on your to-do list, it could free up energy for something more interesting or invigorating at home or in the community.

At the beginning of the week: What have you been putting off? Why? How has delaying the task affected your attention to other chores, to other people? How has it affected your mood?

At the end of the week: How did you feel once you accomplished something you've been putting off? Did checking this to-do off your list free up your time or energy? What will you take on next?

Only use your phone for texting and calling this week.

Many of us automatically pull out our phones when we have a few extra seconds to spare during the day—say, in the elevator, at the bus stop, or waiting in line at the grocery store. And because of that, we risk missing out on the community around us.

At the beginning of the week: What is your relationship like with your phone? Do you ever use it to disengage from others or to relieve boredom or anxiety? Write about your daytime phone use, and think about what might be driving your habits.

At the end of the week: Were you able to reserve your phone for texting and making calls? How did you fill the time you would usually spend on your device? If you found the practice beneficial to your outlook, productivity, or interactions with others, consider extending it to next week too.

We must be purposely kind and generous or we miss the best part of existence. The heart that goes out of itself gets large and full of joy. This is the great secret of the inner life. We do ourselves the most good by doing something for others.

HORACE MANN (1796–1859),
EDUCATIONAL REFORMER AND POLITICIAN

Introduce yourself to someone whom you see regularly but have never met.

There are many people with whom we cross paths on a regular basis but never take the extra step to learn their names or interact. They might be the barista who crafts your morning latte, the cashier at your local grocery store, or even a neighbor who you see regularly on your evening run. By making a connection, you'll be fostering a friendlier, more open community.

At the beginning of the week: Do you tend to initiate conversation with strangers, or do you tend toward shyness? Think about your typical day and the people you see with whom you do not normally engage. What could be holding you back?

At the end of the week: Did you introduce yourself to someone you see regularly but haven't met? What was the interaction like? Do you feel inspired to introduce yourself to another person you see frequently but don't know?

Give everyone the benefit of the doubt this week.

How would your life be different if you went into each interaction with the assumption that everyone you meet has your best interest at heart? Since you can't know another's thoughts and feelings, you might as well assume the best first.

At the beginning of the week: Consider how you enter into interactions with others. Do you tend to be suspicious and impatient or open and relaxed? How does the thought of doing this exercise make you feel?

At the end of the week: Revisit your interactions from the past week. Were you successful in trying to assume the best? Write about how it felt. If you weren't always able to give people the benefit of the doubt, why not? Describe an incident in which you weren't able to do this and how you might approach a similar situation differently.

This week, donate food to someone who needs it.

Go online to find what your local food bank needs, then drop off a bagful of groceries. Or go through your pantry and find any extra food you can donate. By providing hungry people with a meal, you'll be helping your community in a very direct and essential way.

At the beginning of the week: Do you donate food on a regular basis? What inspires you to do so? If you don't regularly make food donations, why not?

At the end of the week: Did you make a donation of food this week? How did donating food make you feel? What impact do you think your contribution will have?

Pull a thread here and you'll find it's attached to the rest of the world.

NADEEM ASLAM (B. 1966), WRITER

Write a letter to someone whose work you've enjoyed or admired.

Sometimes we forget that people we don't know personally are real people who appreciate being appreciated. Whether it's an author of a book you read recently, a politician who implemented a policy you support, or a musician whose music you love, let that person know.

At the beginning of the week: List five people whose work you've appreciated. Out of these five people, who would you like to write to and why? Write a draft of your letter here.

At the end of the week: How did it feel to express your thanks to someone whose work you admire? Even if you never hear from the recipient, what impact do you imagine your note will have on them? If you enjoyed this exercise, consider writing letters to other people whose work you appreciate.

Every day, find a quiet space where you can sit. Set a timer. During that time, focus on your breath.

If you're still not sure about developing a meditation practice, start with five minutes and sit quietly every day. Or if you have been practicing and you want to try something new, focus on your heart beating, the physical sensations of your body, or the sounds around you.

At the beginning of the week: Have you been able to make time to meditate? If not, what's stopped you? If you have been practicing, write about your experience and if it has had any impact on the rest of your day or week.

At the end of the week: Did you sit quietly each day this week? What thoughts, feelings, and physical sensations did you experience? Do you think you will continue this practice? Why or why not?

Nothing can bring you peace but yourself.

RALPH WALDO EMERSON (1803–1882), POET

Share a meal with someone new this week.

Perhaps you cook every day for your family, or maybe you tend to go solo for supper. Whatever your routine, this week add a new person to it, whether it's inviting an acquaintance you'd like to know better over for dinner or taking a coworker out to eat for a lunchtime meeting. Food can be so much more than just fuel—it can be a source of joy, a means to express creativity, and a way to connect with others.

At the beginning of the week: Who is someone new you'd like to share a meal with? How does the thought of doing this exercise make you feel? Write about a recipe or restaurant you've been wanting to try, and why you'd like to share it with someone.

At the end of the week: Did you dine with someone new this week? If so, write about the experience—the invitation, the meal itself, the conversation.

Find the silver lining in tough situations this week.

You might not always be able to control what happens in your life. But you do have some power over how you interpret life's ups and downs. When something doesn't go as planned, ask yourself: What can I learn from this? What good might come of this?

At the beginning of the week: Do you consider yourself an optimist or a pessimist? Provide examples of either. What might be your biggest challenge in finding a silver lining this week?

At the end of the week: Were you able to see the silver lining in tough situations? What did you learn about yourself or about others if you did so? How did the exercise influence your thoughts and actions this week?

For me, I am driven by two main philosophies: know more today about the world than I knew yesterday and lessen the suffering of others. You'd be surprised how far that gets you.

NEIL DEGRASSE TYSON (B. 1958), ASTROPHYSICIST

Exercise outside every day this week.

A little fresh air and exercise can improve the way you feel and clear your head. Go for a walk, ride your bike, take a hike through the park—by getting outside you might learn something new about your area, meet a new person, or simply have a moment to appreciate the great outdoors.

At the beginning of the week: Do you currently take walks or do other activities outside? How often do you spend time outside, and how does doing so make you feel? If you don't do this form of self-care, why not?

At the end of the week: What was your outdoor activity like this week? How did you feel before, during, and after the exercise? Did it change your outlook or mood in any way?

This week, write a positive review online or find another way to spread the word about a local business you enjoy.

Give five stars on Yelp, rave about a restaurant on Facebook, or simply tell your friends and coworkers about someone whose service you enjoyed. Business owners and employees will be glad to hear that you appreciate them, and you'll guide friends and neighbors to trusted vendors.

At the beginning of the week: List three local businesses whose services you've enjoyed. What specifically do you appreciate about them? Choose one of the businesses and write the rough draft of your digital or verbal praise here.

At the end of the week: Did you give a positive review of a local business this week? How did this exercise make you feel? What do you hope to achieve for the company by doing this?

A single act of kindness throws out roots in all directions, and the roots spring up and make new trees.

FREDERICK WILLIAM FABER (1814–1863),
REVEREND AND HYMN WRITER

This week, give up one thing that you usually purchase daily and donate the money you save to charity.

Skip the stop at the coffee shop for a morning latte or bring a bag lunch instead of going out. You might find that you don't miss it all that much—or you may be reminded how much you appreciate that little treat! Even one week's worth of savings can go a long way in helping someone else.

At the beginning of the week: What's a daily purchase that you can give up? Do you think it will be easy or difficult? What charity would you like to donate the money you save to, and why?

At the end of the week: Did you give up one daily purchase? If you did, how did doing so make you feel throughout the week? How much money were you able to donate? If you didn't follow through on the exercise, why not?

Clean up after yourself right away this week.

Wash dishes right after the meal, fold laundry straight out of the dryer, sweep the floor as soon as it gets dirty. It may seem like extra effort in the short run, but in the long run it could save you the time and energy required for putting it off. And perhaps it will give you more time to relax, do an activity you enjoy, or do something extra for someone you love.

At the beginning of the week: Is there a daily chore that you tend to put off? Why? Are you dreading doing this exercise or are you glad to have the extra push to get through your chores?

At the end of the week: Did you clean up after yourself right away this week? If you did, describe what that was like. How did it make you feel? How did it affect your day-to-day life? If you didn't clean up after yourself this week, what do you think prevented you?

Share a positive news story this week.

Bad news is just a click away. But reminding ourselves that there are people doing good in the world can give hope and inspire someone to take positive action. Send a good story to a friend in an e-mail, write about it in your blog, or clip it from a newspaper and stick it to your fridge for your family to see.

At the beginning of the week: Are you more frequently drawn to negative news stories or positive ones? How do you feel after reading them? Where might you look for some good news to share?

At the end of the week: How did sharing a positive news story this week make you feel? Write about the article, and why you chose it. How did other people respond? Would you consider continuing to seek out and share similar news stories in the future?

The best way to not feel hopeless is to get up and do something.

BARACK OBAMA (B. 1961), 44TH US PRESIDENT

Buy at least one item from a local source or small business owner this week.

Not everyone has access to food grown or items made nearby, or businesses owned by local people. This week, buy produce from a local farm, drop by a neighborhood bookstore versus a national chain, or go to an antique shop instead of a big-box furniture store. You'll be supporting your community by spending your time and money in it.

At the beginning of the week: Do you have easy access to locally produced food or products or locally owned businesses? Who would you like to purchase from or support, and why?

At the end of the week: How did buying local this week affect your lifestyle? How might it have influenced someone in your community? If you were unable to find a local item to purchase this week, where might you look next week to support your community's businesses?

Every day, find a quiet space where you can sit. Set a timer. During that time, focus on your breath.

If you're working on developing a meditation practice, consistency is key. If you haven't started yet, begin with five minutes and sit quietly every day. If you have been meditating and you're interested in a challenge, add some extra time to your practice.

At the beginning of the week: If you've been practicing, write about your experience. If you haven't been practicing, write about the experience of *not* practicing.

At the end of the week: Did you sit quietly each day this week? What thoughts, feelings, and physical sensations did you experience? Would you consider continuing this practice?

If I am not for myself, who will be for me? But if I am only for myself, who am I? If not now, when?

HILLEL THE ELDER (110 BCE–10 CE), RABBI

Offer a sincere thank-you.

Sometimes we forget to say thank you, or we say thank you all the time but on autopilot. What would it be like to really pay attention when you're expressing your gratitude?

At the beginning of the week: When, where, and how do you usually say thank you? Would doing this exercise alter your MO? Who do you think would most benefit from hearing your thanks, and why?

At the end of the week: Did you offer a sincere thank-you this week? Was it different from the usual way you express yourself? How might expressing your appreciation more often benefit your relationships, whether personal or professional?

Donate money to a charitable organization this week.

Pick an issue or issues that are meaningful to you—human rights, climate change, education, for example—and write a check. It can be for a small sum, but give enough to push you out of your financial comfort zone. You may also consider spreading that amount across a few charitable organizations. Because it's likely that you'll be fine if you give a little more than is comfortable, and even that little bit can increase your impact.

At the beginning of the week: What is the maximum amount of money you'd be comfortable with donating? How does the prospect of stepping out of your financial comfort zone make you feel? Write about the issue(s) you chose and why.

At the end of the week: Did you donate money this week? How did pushing yourself out of your financial comfort zone feel?

For it is in giving that we receive.

FRANCIS OF ASSISI (1181–1226),
FRIAR, PREACHER, AND SAINT

Open your mind by watching a different news channel, listening to a different podcast or radio program, or reading a different newspaper.

Most of us like to get information that validates our opinions. By checking out a different source, you might broaden your understanding of an issue and an opposing point of view. That might help you find more compassion—or at least patience—for people you disagree with.

At the beginning of the week: What sorts of news do you tend to consume? In what ways does it confirm your established opinions? Write about an issue you feel strongly about, and what difficulties you might have in understanding a different point of view.

At the end of the week: What was it like to go to a different source for news? Write about something you heard or read that surprised you or made you reconsider your point of view.

Pick up someone's tab this week.

Pay for a stranger's coffee, give a grocery store clerk twenty dollars toward the next customer's purchase, or pay the toll for the car behind you. It's a small expense that can bring joy to another.

At the beginning of the week: Where do you think the opportunity to pay someone's tab might come up? Do you feel comfortable doing this exercise? How would you feel if someone paid your tab?

At the end of the week: Did you pick up someone's tab this week? How did they react? Would you do this again? Why or why not?

Never look down on anybody unless you're helping them up.

JESSE JACKSON (B. 1941), CIVIL RIGHTS ACTIVIST, REVEREND, AND POLITICIAN

Go out of your way to be friendly to your coworkers or neighbors this week.

It's easy to get stuck in a routine and keep your nose to the grindstone. But what if you stopped for a chat with a coworker in the break room or engaged with your neighbor instead of dashing inside? Making an extra effort to connect with those around you can be a cure for an everyday rut—for both you and them.

At the beginning of the week: Who in your life do you tend to rush past? Why? How does the thought of stopping to engage them make you feel? What might you gain by fostering a connection with them?

At the end of the week: Did you go out of your way to be friendly this week? How did it affect your time, mood, and behavior? Write about an interesting interaction you had.

Make extra time for yourself every day this week.

It's easy to forget about self-care if it's not on your to-do list. This week, make sure you set aside some extra time, even if you have to put it on your calendar. Whether it's ten minutes for reading before bed, a half hour for a hot bath, or an hour to call your best friend—whatever it is, do something that is nurturing for you. Because you can't help someone else fill their tank if you are running on empty.

At the beginning of the week: What do you think about the idea of "self-care"? Does it seem narcissistic, essential, selfish, affirming? Do you tend to make time for self-care? If not, what prevents you from doing so? Write down five possible self-care activities (or nonactivities) for this week.

At the end of the week: Did you make extra time for yourself this week? What did you choose to do? How did it make you feel? If you didn't, why not?

You only have what you give.

ISABEL ALLENDE (B. 1942), WRITER

This week, go through your closet and donate anything you don't need.

A rule of thumb is: If you haven't worn it in one year, you probably never will. Those clothes and shoes that are taking up space in your closet? Someone else might actually use them.

At the beginning of the week: Do you wear every item in your closet, or do you have clothes you haven't worn in a while? Write about your relationship to your clothing, and what impact it might have if you gave some clothing away.

At the end of the week: What emotions did you experience while choosing which clothes to give away? Was it easy for you or was it hard to let items go? How did you feel while giving the clothing away, knowing that it could end up in the hands of someone who needs it?

Act like someone in your life whose kindness you admire.

It can be anyone—the friendly mail carrier, your spouse, your late grandfather. Each day, when faced with a challenging or new situation, ask yourself: What would that person do?

At the beginning of the week: Who is someone whose kindness you admire? Write about some instances when you witnessed or received their kindness. What specific behaviors would you like to emulate?

At the end of the week: Write about an interaction in which you asked *What would that person do*? before acting this week. How did that interaction make you feel? What, if any, response did you get?

With a little reason and much heart, one can change many things, or move mountains.

ALBERT SCHWEITZER (1875–1965),
THEOLOGIAN, PHILOSOPHER, AND PHYSICIAN

Eat like a vegetarian this week.

Without judging yourself, your diet, or anyone else, stick to plant-based foods this week. Though it may not be right for everyone in the long term, eating a vegetarian diet can have a positive environmental and ethical impact, as well as improve your health.

At the beginning of the week: Roughly how much meat do you consume in a week? Will this exercise change your day-to-day life? If so, how does the prospect of doing this exercise make you feel? If not, what is your motivation for not eating meat?

At the end of the week: Did you eat like a vegetarian this week? How did doing so (or not doing so) make you feel? Would you consider altering your diet in the long term, even in a small way, such as giving up meat one day a week?

This week, as soon as you get home, put away your phone.

Your phone is an extraordinary tool. But sometimes it can distract during dinner with your roommates or family, take up valuable time that could be used for finishing chores, or get in the way of a hobby or more soothing self-care. This week, put your phone away and see what happens with the free time that creates.

At the beginning of the week: Estimate how much time you spend on your phone during the evenings. Does your phone ever distract or detract from important relationships or activities? Write about your phone use, and what you might do during the extra time at home this week when you are phone-free.

At the end of the week: Did you put away your phone every evening? What did you do during that extra time? What challenges to following through on this activity did you encounter?

One's life has value so long as one attributes value to the life of others, by means of love, friendship, indignation, and compassion.

SIMONE DE BEAUVOIR (1908–1986), WRITER, PHILOSOPHER, AND SOCIAL THEORIST

Every day, find a quiet space where you can just sit. Set a timer. During that time, focus on your breath.

If you're still not sure about developing a meditation practice, start with five minutes and sit quietly every day. Or if you have been practicing and you're interested in a challenge, try counting your breaths for the duration of the time. If you lose track, begin again at one.

At the beginning of the week: If you just started meditating, what was your experience like? If you've been practicing, has your experience changed in any way?

At the end of the week: Did you sit quietly each day this week? What thoughts, feelings, and physical sensations did you experience? Would you consider continuing this practice?

Love makes labor light.

J. G. HOLLAND (1819–1881), NOVELIST AND POET

Buy nothing this week.

Prepare yourself by getting the essentials at the beginning of the week. Then buy nothing—you might gain a new understanding of the difference between what you need *and what you* want. *Plus reassessing your needs might help to free up money for travel, self-care, or contributing to a cause you care about.*

At the beginning of the week: What are some of your most regular weekly purchases? Which of these are necessary, like food and toiletries, and which are nonessential, like a manicure or an outing to the movies? How does the thought of planning ahead and then buying nothing make you feel?

At the end of the week: Write about a time this week when you wanted to make a purchase but refrained. What was that like for you? Will you immediately make the purchase next week or will you hold back still? How might this practice feel for someone who has less than you financially?

Start a conversation with a stranger this week.

There are an infinite number of fascinating people in the world. So shelve your fear or hesitation, make some friendly eye contact, and talk to someone new.

At the beginning of the week: How does the thought of doing this exercise make you feel? Is this an exercise that will take you out of your comfort zone, or do you like talking with strangers? Describe how you usually interact with people you don't know.

At the end of the week: How did you feel before, during, and after your conversation with a stranger? What did you learn about them? Did you have anything in common?

Love is a fruit in season at all times, and within reach of every hand.

MOTHER TERESA (1910–1997), NUN,
NOBEL PEACE PRIZE WINNER, AND SAINT

Give to the homeless this week.

Homelessness is an incredibly complex issue, and sometimes it's easier to pass by a panhandler than it is to acknowledge or help them. If you encounter homeless people in your daily life, this week make a point of giving change, packaged food, clean socks, or hand wipes to someone living on the street. If you don't usually encounter people who are homeless, collect your change and then make a donation to a food bank or homeless shelter in the equivalent amount.

At the beginning of the week: What are your beliefs about homelessness or poverty and the people who experience them? What are your beliefs about charity for the homeless or the poor? How does the prospect of doing this exercise make you feel?

At the end of the week: Did you give change, food, or goods to someone living on the street or make a donation to a food bank or shelter this week? What was the interaction like? Would you consider doing it again?

Devote some time to a new activity each day this week.

That hobby you've always wanted to try but never had the time? There's no time like the present. And you never know where a new adventure might take you and whom you might meet along the way.

At the beginning of the week: What is an activity that you've always wanted to try but haven't? What has held you back? What obstacles might you have to overcome? In what ways might it expand your horizons?

At the end of the week: Did you devote some time to a new project this week? How were you able to make time for it? How did doing so make you feel? If you didn't, why not?

Pick up litter in your neighborhood this week.

You are as responsible for the environment as anyone else. Even spending ten minutes picking up litter makes a difference—you'll be contributing to the beauty and health of the environment that you and the animals, plants, and people in your neighborhood share.

At the beginning of the week: Do you tend to take personal responsibility for the area in which you live, or do you think that others will? What are the short- and long-term benefits of assuming responsibility for the environment?

At the end of the week: Did you pick up litter in your neighborhood this week? Describe what you did and what it was like for you. Is this a practice you would consider repeating on a weekly or biweekly basis?

The more he does for others, the more he has of his own. The more he gives to others, the more he is increased.

LAOZI (604–531 BCE), PHILOSOPHER AND WRITER

Tell a friend or acquaintance what you like about them.

Maybe your friend has no idea that his smile makes you happy. Perhaps your coworker would love to know that you admire her cleverness. Whatever it is you like about someone, this is the week to tell them.

At the beginning of the week: Do you tend to give compliments freely, or are you more reserved in expressing yourself in this way? How do you feel about *receiving* compliments? List ten people in your life and one thing you like about each of them.

At the end of the week: Did you tell a friend or acquaintance what you like about them this week? How do you think doing so influenced their day? Who is next up on your list and why?

Ask for help this week.

No matter how great the burden, you don't have to shoulder it alone. Asking others for help gives them a chance to show you that they care.

At the beginning of the week: How do you feel about asking for help? Are you comfortable, hesitant, eager, unsure? Make a list of five things you need help with this week. What kind of reaction do you anticipate getting when you ask for a hand?

At the end of the week: Was asking for help this week easy or hard? Did the response you received encourage you to ask for help in the future or did it discourage you from asking again?

Volunteer your time this week.

Do you have a special skill or strength you could use to help others? Whether it's helping a child with her homework, addressing envelopes for a nonprofit's fund-raiser, or running an errand for an elderly neighbor, your effort will be appreciated.

At the beginning of the week: Write about a skill or strength you could use to help others. What might be the best way to use it? Which community would most benefit from your help?

At the end of the week: Write about your volunteer experience. How did sharing your skills make you feel? How was your participation received? If you didn't volunteer or don't plan to again, how might you overcome what's preventing you from doing so?

The best way to cheer yourself is to try to cheer somebody else up.

MARK TWAIN (1835–1910), WRITER

Every day, find a quiet space where you can just sit. Set a timer. During that time, focus on your breath.

If you're still not sure about developing a meditation practice, start with five minutes and sit every day. Or if you have been practicing, choose the method you like best and add some extra time to your practice.

At the beginning of the week: Write about how this practice has—or has not—been going.

At the end of the week: Did you sit quietly each day this week? What thoughts, feelings, and physical sensations did you experience? Would you consider continuing this practice for the long term?

Commit a random act of kindness every day.

You can repeat an exercise from this journal, come up with your own, or do something kind spontaneously, when the opportunity arises. You have the power to make the world a better place: love first and act accordingly.

Consider the various exercises you took part in. Which exercises had the most impact in your life? How do you feel the quality of your life has improved or been altered? Which exercises will you consider continuing in the future?

About the Author

Before committing to the world of books, Anna Katz had a career in mental health and social services. As an editor and writer at Girl Friday Productions, she has worked with *National Geographic Kids*, Deloitte, and Pokémon, among others. Her newest book, *Swimming Holes of Washington*, will be published by Mountaineers Books in 2018.